Genre Expository Text

I0902689

Essential Question
What can scientists reveal about ancient civilizations?

THE ANCIENT CITY OF UR

BY MARIA GILL

INTRODUCTION

In 1922, an **archaeologist** named Leonard Woolley **embarked** on a journey to southern Iraq. Woolley was going to study the ruins of a tower called a ziggurat, which had been built centuries before. At the time the ziggurat was erected, this area of southern Iraq was called Sumer. The tower had been an important place in the city-state of Ur. It is known as the Great Ziggurat of Ur.

Woolley began digging near the ruins. During these **excavations**, it was discovered that Ur had once been near the Euphrates River. Now the river was 10 miles (16 kilometers) away. Civilizations near rivers often **flourish**. These civilizations do well because people can utilize the river for transportation and to irrigate crops.

MODERN-DAY IRAQ

Ur was located near the Euphrates River. Today the river is about 10 miles from Ur.

Woolley and his team dug two large **trenches** near the ziggurat. In the first trench, they found graves and gold. However, Woolley knew that he and his workers were too inexperienced to excavate graves successfully. They decided not to explore this first site yet.

In the second trench, they found the ruins of an extensive wall and several buildings. This was one of the most exciting discoveries of the twentieth century.

The Great Ziggurat of Ur is one of Iraq's most important sites.

In 1923, Woolley and the workers began to **meticulously** examine the ruins of the ziggurat. The building was made of bricks. The bricks on the outside were sealed with a tar-like substance. This seal protected the ziggurat from floods.

THE GREAT ZIGGURAT OF UR

The ziggurat had three levels, with brick staircases between them. Woolley noticed that the walls were not straight. They were slightly **sloped**, or slanted, which made the structure appear very strong. This design showed that Ur was more modern than other city-states from that time. It was a very advanced civilization.

ZIGGURATS

No one knows exactly what ziggurats were used for. The people who lived in the area believed that the gods came from the mountains. Maybe the ziggurats were built to look like mountains. Each ziggurat had a temple on top. Maybe the people built ziggurats to lift up the temples so that the gods could easily come to Earth.

THE FIRST TEMPLE

Woolley found a small building near the ziggurat. Writing on the structure showed that it had been a sacred temple called E-nun-mah.

Woolley discovered that the walls of the temple had been constructed much earlier than the floors. This made him think that there might be another level below the floor. Then his workers dug below the bricks. They found gold beads, earrings, and other jewelry.

King Ur-Nammu built the temple of E-nun-mah.

THE HIGH PRIESTESS

Woolley's team found two more buildings near E-nun-mah. One was named E-dub-lal-mah. This structure contained a **shrine** where priestesses, or women who were religious leaders, worshipped Nannar, the moon god. The other building was called E-gi-par. It was the **residence**, or home, of a high priestess.

The archaeologists found several clay **tablets** in the buildings. A teacher had written a sentence on one side of a tablet. A student had attempted to copy it on the other side. Another tablet looked like a spelling book and was labeled "the property of the boys' class." Woolley believed that the high priestess had taught lessons in those rooms.

Woolley found benches, altars, and tables in the excavations.

In the shrine in E-dub-lal-mah, Woolley's team found a statue of King Dungi. He was the son of Ur-Nammu, who **reigned** about 4,000 years ago. The workers also found a stone weapon that was older than the statue. They found clay tablets that were not as old as the statue.

Woolley wondered why there were objects from different times in one room. This was an **intriguing** puzzle. Woolley found the answer on some clay cylinders. Writing on the cylinders described each item. The room had been a museum.

STOP AND CHECK

Why did Woolley think that there might be a level below the floors of the first temple?

The clay cylinders were labels from the world's oldest known museum.

CHAPTER 2

AN ADVANCED CIVILIZATION

Woolley's excavations revealed many interesting things about the city of Ur.

CITY OF TREES

Woolley investigated narrow slits in the first level of the ziggurat wall. Nearby, Woolley found a building that had been damaged by tree branches. He thought that people might have grown trees on the ziggurat. The slits were probably part of an **irrigation** system. They had been used to water the trees.

Woolley also uncovered signs that the residents of Ur had irrigated crops using canals and dams. The water came from the Euphrates River.

Woolley guided each excavation carefully.

TRADING ALONG THE RIVER

Woolley learned that business people of Ur transported goods along the river. They recorded their trade **transactions** on clay tablets. They also recorded the sales and **leases** of land.

Woolley found **exquisite** jewelry with gems. The gems were from other places, so the people of Ur must have traded for them. These discoveries were more signs that Ur was an advanced civilization.

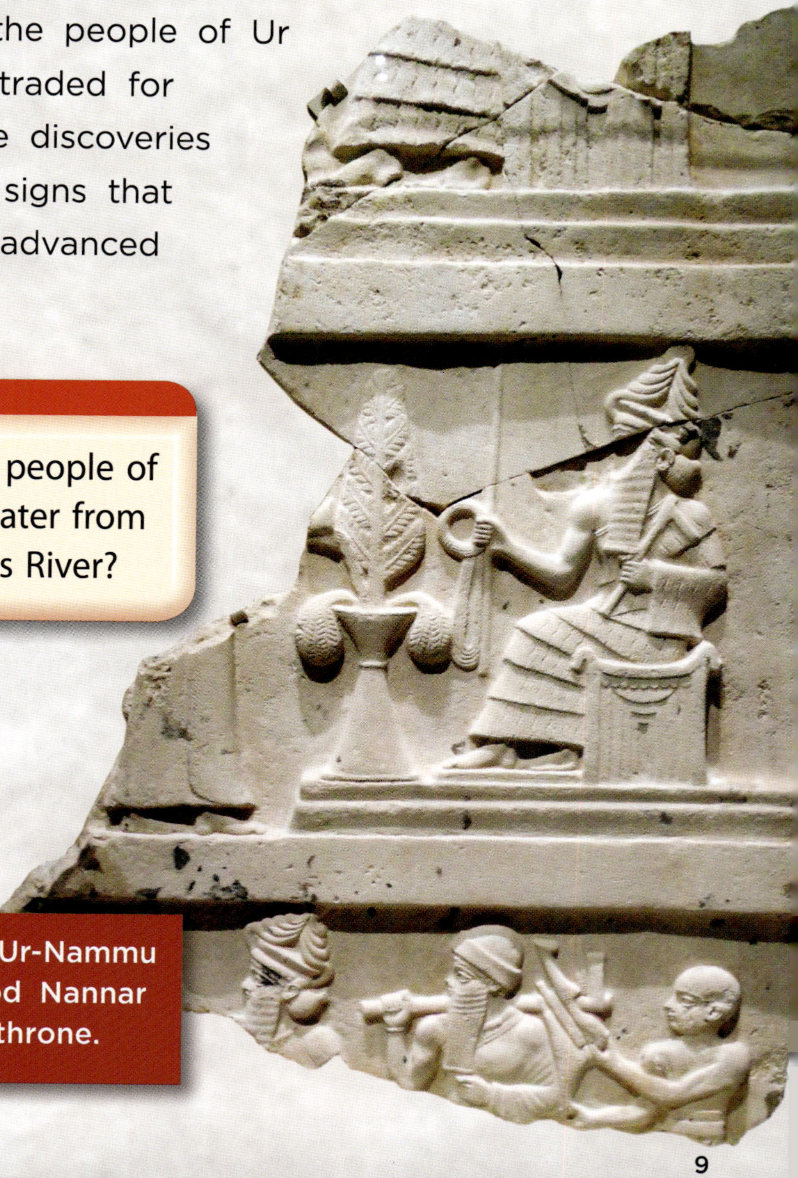

STOP AND CHECK

How did the people of Ur use the water from the Euphrates River?

The Stele of Ur-Nammu shows the god Nannar seated on a throne.

Inscribed bricks give archaeologists useful information.

CLUES IN CLAY

King Ur-Nammu began building the ziggurat about 4,000 years ago. His son, King Dungi, and other kings added to it later. About 1,400 years after King Ur-Nammu, a 6-foot-high wall was constructed around the sacred buildings. It was called the Temenos Wall.

We know this information because it was written on clay cylinders. The people of Ur **inscribed** the cylinders by scratching wet clay with a **reed**. The clay was then baked in the sun.

The people of Ur used an ancient writing system called cuneiform. The word *cuneiform* comes from the Latin word *cuneus*, meaning "wedge." The reeds made a wedge shape on the clay tablets.

STOP AND CHECK

How do we know that King Dungi and other kings added to the ziggurat?

HOW CUNEIFORM DEVELOPED

Cuneiform is one of the oldest written languages. It first appeared in Sumer more than 5,000 years ago. Cuneiform used pictographs, or pictures. Each pictograph stood for an object or idea.

Name	Earliest Outline Characters		Archaic Cuneiform	Late Babylonian
	Pictograph	4500 B.C.E.	2500 B.C.E.	500 B.C.E.
Day			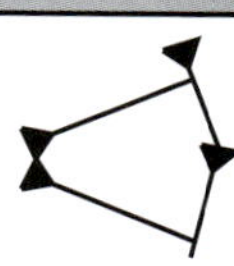	
Hand			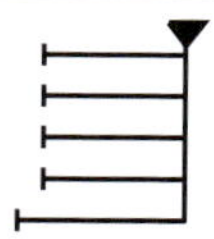	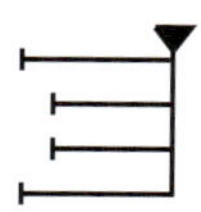
Bird	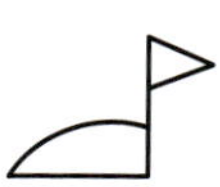			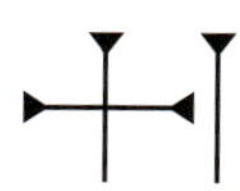
Fish				

THE GRAVES

By 1927, Woolley's workers had improved their excavation skills. They were ready to excavate the graves they had found in 1922.

COMMONERS' GRAVES

The team first found hundreds of graves belonging to **commoners**. The commoners were the local village people.

A thin line of white powder marked each grave. The powder was what was left of reed mats that had lined the graves. Graves often contained jewelry, tools, or inscribed cylinders. Sometimes there were also offerings to the dead. The offerings could be food, drink, weapons, or tools.

In March 1927, the workers found a large pit lined with limestone. Woolley was surprised. The builders would have had to travel more than 30 miles (50 kilometers) to get the limestone. Why would the builders go to so much trouble?

Woolley got the answer when the team found two rooms built from stone near the pit. There was a ramp cut into the **bedrock**. The ramp led from the rooms to a tomb that had been built for **royalty**, or the kings and queens.

PRINCE MES-KALAM-DUG'S TREASURES

Prince Mes-kalam-dug's grave contained tools, bowls, and weapons made from copper and gold.

Inside the coffin was a silver belt with a gold dagger. There were also a gold headdress, a gold helmet, and lots of jewelry. The prince held a heavy gold bowl in his hands.

This helmet in Prince Mes-kalam-dug's grave was made from beaten gold.

A SURPRISING DISCOVERY

By early 1928, the workers had dug 26 feet below the surface of the ground. Here they found a **shaft** made out of mud bricks. Below the shaft was a pit, with another pit below it.

The lowest pit contained the bodies of 6 men and 68 women. Woolley called this the Great Death Pit.

This illustration shows people and animals walking into the burial shaft.

Woolley believed these people had been servants to royalty. They may have thought it was a **privilege** to die with their rulers.

However, Woolley did not find a royal tomb **chamber**, or special room, connected to the Great Death Pit. He thought grave robbers may have taken the bodies and treasure.

STOP AND CHECK

What did the team find in the commoners' graves?

TREASURES FROM THE ROYAL TOMBS OF UR

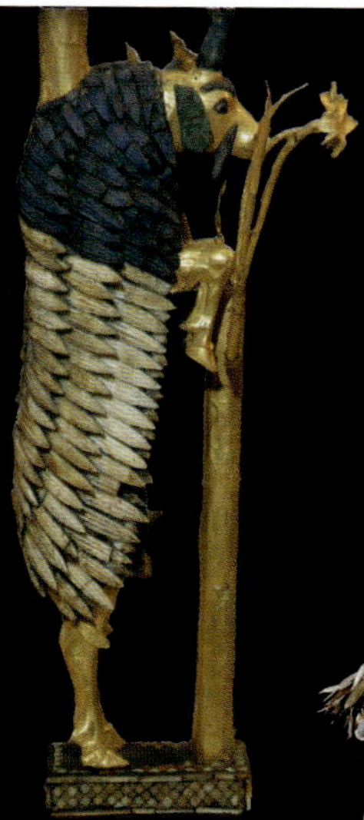

This statue of a ram was found in the Great Death Pit.

Queen Puabi wore this headdress. It is made of gold and jewels.

This gold wreath contains gems.

CONCLUSION

The ruins of Ur are located far from modern-day villages. This distance from people, as well as the hot climate, may have helped protect the ruins.

Woolley's camp contained a large house with a generator for electricity. The workers lived in a village 4 miles (6.5 kilometers) away. The laborers' children brought them their lunches. Then the children hunted for treasures, too.

Woolley's wife Katharine also worked at Ur.

Woolley was a **methodical** archaeologist. Through his careful, orderly excavations, he found objects that were as beautiful as the treasures of Egypt. He also discovered a lot about the residents of Ur. He and his workers learned about the people of Ur's writing, **commerce**, and daily lives.

Woolley's excavations also help us understand Ur's **demise**. The city declined when the Euphrates River changed course around 2,600 years ago. The people could not irrigate their crops or transport their goods. People began to move away. The great city was slowly covered by sand.

The world is a richer place because of Woolley's discoveries.

The Great Ziggurat of Ur was rebuilt in the 1960s and 1970s.

Respond to Reading

Summarize

Use details from *The Ancient City of Ur* to summarize what you learned about this ancient civilization. Your graphic organizer may help you.

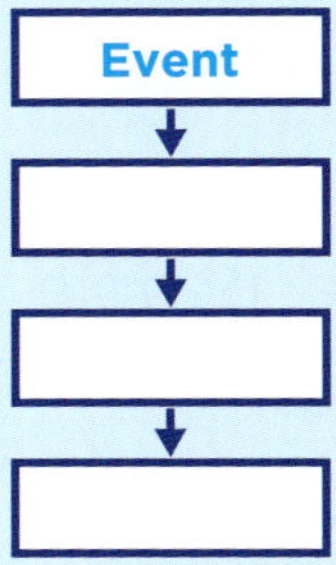

Text Evidence

1. In Chapter 3, how does the author show the order of the events in the excavation? **SEQUENCE**

2. Find the word *advanced* on page 4. What clues help you to figure out the word's meaning? **VOCABULARY**

3. Write about the first discovery in Chapter 1 that led Woolley to think Ur was very advanced? **WRITE ABOUT READING**

Genre Mystery

Compare Texts

Read about a girl who helps solve an archaeological mystery.

THE GAME

Sarah sighed when she saw her parents examining the small clay balls they had found. She knew they wouldn't be leaving the excavation early.

Sarah wasn't having much fun in the ancient city of Çatalhöyük in Turkey. She liked spending weekends with her parents in Istanbul. The weather was very hot, and their hotel in Istanbul had a huge swimming pool.

Sarah's parents had said that the clay balls had **intrinsic** value. They were an important find no matter what they had been used for. However, Sarah knew her parents wouldn't leave the dig site until they'd learned more.

Then Sarah had an idea. Maybe she could solve the mystery of the clay balls. Then they could go back to Istanbul and swim in the pool.

Sarah went into the room where artifacts were stored. She noticed some bone rings from a burial site. Sarah couldn't imagine wearing a ring made of bone.

Next she looked at a mural that showed people kneeling in the sand. She wondered what the people were doing.

Sarah went outside for some fresh air. A young girl was walking past, so Sarah said hi to her.

The girl smiled and said her name, which was Sena. The girls sat down and Sena taught Sarah to play a Turkish game of marbles called *gülle*. Something about the game seemed familiar to Sarah.

After a while, Sarah said good-bye to Sena and went back to the dig site. On the way, she realized something important.

"I think the people in that mural are playing a game," she said to her mother in the room of artifacts.

Sarah described the game that Sena had taught her. Then she noticed her mother's ring, which reminded her of the bone rings.

"The clay balls!" Sarah cried. "People didn't have marbles back then, so they could have used clay balls to play the game. It's just like how we wear metal rings now instead of rings made from bone."

"That's a good theory," her mother said. "Let's talk about it on the way to Istanbul."

Sarah skipped out of the room. "Yahoo! Swimming pool, here I come!"

Make Connections

How does Sarah solve the mystery of the clay balls? **ESSENTIAL QUESTION**

How do people learn about ancient civilizations in *The Ancient City of Ur* and *The Game*? **TEXT TO TEXT**

Glossary

archaeologist *(ahr-kee-AHL-uh-jist)* a person who studies ancient civilizations by looking at the things left behind ***(page 2)***

commerce *(KAHM-uhrs)* buying and selling of goods, especially between different places and on a large scale ***(page 17)***

demise *(di-MIGHZ)* ending or failure ***(page 17)***

leases *(LEES-iz)* agreements to rent property ***(page 9)***

privilege *(PRIV-lij)* a favor that is granted to some but not others ***(page 15)***

reed *(reed)* a stiff grass ***(page 10)***

reigned *(raynd)* ruled over an area, usually by a pharaoh, emperor, king, or queen ***(page 7)***

shaft *(shaft)* an opening or passage straight down through the floors of a building ***(page 14)***

shrine *(shrighn)* a place that is considered sacred; where people go to pay respects to a god ***(page 6)***

tablets *(TAB-lits)* small slabs for writing on ***(page 6)***

transactions *(tran-ZAK-shuhnz)* business deals ***(page 9)***

trenches *(TRENCH-iz)* long, narrow ditches ***(page 3)***

Index

Social Studies

Purpose To research how ancient cultures used the resources in their areas

What to Do

Step 1 Work with a partner. Find out about an ancient site that is being excavated today. Find out what natural resources are in the area.

Step 2 What objects have been found at the site? What materials were used to make the objects? Did ancient people find the materials in their area, or did they bring the materials from somewhere else?

Step 3 Share what you learned with the class. Explain why the objects were important to the people in that area.